GENDER TROUBLE COUPLETS

BEFORE YOU START TO READ THIS BOOK, take this moment to think about making a donation to punctum books, an independent non-profit press,

@ https://punctumbooks.com/support/

If you're reading the e-book, you can click on the image below to go directly to our donations site. Any amount, no matter the size, is appreciated and will help us to keep our ship of fools afloat. Contributions from dedicated readers will also help us to keep our commons open and to cultivate new work that can't find a welcoming port elsewhere. Our adventure is not possible without your support.

Vive la Open Access.

Fig. 1. Hieronymus Bosch, *Ship of Fools* (1490–1500)

An excerpt of this work was previously published in *Lunch*: http://www.lunchreview.org/gender-trouble-couplets-volume-1.

First published in 2019 by punctum books, Earth, Milky Way.
https://punctumbooks.com

ISBN-13: 978-1-950192-51-9 (print)
ISBN-13: 978-1-950192-52-6 (ePDF)

DOI: 10.21983/P3.0266.1.00

LCCN: 2019952284
Library of Congress Cataloging Data is available from the Library of Congress

Book design: Vincent W.J. van Gerven Oei

HIC SVNT MONSTRA

A.W. STROUSE's

GENDER TROUBLE

COUPLETS

VOLUME 1

Ⓟ

CONTENTS

For Henry Berman Shapiro

Tu se' lo mio maestro e 'l mio autore,
tu se' solo colui da cu' io tolsi
lo bello stilo che m'ha fatto onore.

Preface

Like an interior design collaboration between Michel Houellebecq and Martha Stewart, putting together a medieval verse form and queer theory is not only magnificent and original, it breathes the rarefied air that hipsters are trying to reach in vain when they turn, after vinyl, to cassette tapes. A.W. Strouse's short commentary on the first chapter of Judith Butler's monumental volume *Gender Trouble* is not only original and fully unexpected, it's sublime.

By short commentary, I mean quite technically the learned medieval form used by Latinate and Islamicate cultures who inherited it from Hellenized Romans and Jews in late-antiquity Alexandria, or from Greek schoolmasters in Byzantium. In medieval reading practice, three types of commentary are common. The middle commentary is what we would call today a translation or modernization. The long commentary explicates all the difficulties and nuances of the text, line by line. It is similar to the modern companion, or the full set of footnotes. It is especially common for legal or the most popular literary texts, such as Ovid's *Heroides*. In the age of print, it was often set in the three margins around the original text, which was printed in the center. It is usually twice or three times longer, often many more, and it dwarfs the original text on the page, while still preserving the hierarchy of values. The page distribution, with the original text in the center and in larger print, makes it look like a precious jewel in a properly humble setting. The short commentary, naturally, is the summary of the text. The present, succulently original volume, is a short commentary in verse. Verse form was not unusual for medieval commentaries of all three types. The reader will feel like they've stepped into a time machine, taking the most beloved queer theorist with them, to disembark in Paris or Oxford or Venice, circa 1290, to have a drink with Roger Bacon or Dante, or maybe Marco Polo.

Why put one of the most famous and still one of the most urgently relevant critical theory texts of the 1990s into a form not used since Petrarch studied at Bologna? A form later reserved for teaching reluctant children manners, as in:

The Goops they talk while eating,
And loud and fast they chew;
And that is why I'm glad that I
Am not a Goop—are you?

For a very good reason, indeed. Not only is this verse version of Butler's immortal, slender volume good fun, it will also help the students digest and remember the turns of Butler's argument. As we all know, Butler writes like a congenial, more elastic friend of Derrida: very down to earth, but nearly impossible to recall at length if you are reading her for the first time. Unless you are a mathematical genius or the kid who, during Spring Break, sits in a café at the University of Chicago discussing neo-communist thought while the rest of your age group has sex on the beach, the level of abstraction may not appeal to you. In terms of cultural references, it's hard to thrill to discussions of Monique Wittig if you've never before read any Wittig, and are later unlikely to do so. As a result, for most mortals, the experience of reading *Gender Trouble* is like alpine skiing: great on paper, difficult in practice.

The thesis of *Gender Trouble*—like all brilliant statements, including $E = mc^2$—is something that, nowadays, even a Catholic small-town twelfth grader knows; that is, gender is performative and its apparently unshakeable stability is not stable, natural, nor original, but it derives its illusion of permanence mostly from sustained repetition. It's a self-stylization with a history. So far, so pedagogically unproblematic. But, as anyone who has ever assigned university or college students *Gender Trouble* to read knows, that assignment works just as great (not) as assigning Lacan's *Seminars*. Take a whole semester to read three of the shorter essays, and it will be the most memorable class that these 1½ students ever took. Assign the whole volume to a large class for this week's discussion, and be prepared to do all the unpacking yourself—unless there is a conservative straight male in the classroom, who will gladly mainsplain it. Later, the vegan student with long hair and felt slippers will confess when they tried to read it out loud, the squirrel outside their window fell asleep with a nut still in her mouth. It's hard to be thrilled by discussions of 1968 lesbians when they are the same age as your grandmother.

This rhymed version solves the problem. It draws a clever cartoon map of the text that is memorable and manageable, navigable and fun. It's a commentary that helps us remember every turn of Butler's thought, and also a work of art that one fondly remembers reading. It's a subversive, secret adventure. If kitsch is art *remis au goût du jour,* remade to suit today's taste, this marvelous poem remakes 1990s feminist philosophy *au goût de* Dante, to the taste of Heloise and Hrabanus Maurus and Jean de Meun. It's not just great art, it's high camp: a loving assassination. It's a marvelous, maximalist *tour de force* that plays with a famously minimalist author. Foucault once said that his generation, so cocky about having revolutionized and reimagined the world, had not invented a single new sexual pleasure. I think it doesn't matter that we haven't, if we are the first to read such a sparkling thing as this poem.

—Anna M. Kłosowska

Gender Trouble Couplets, Volume 1

"Women" as the Subject of Feminism

But must there be a Womankind?
A female Heart and female Mind?
For Feminism to exist
then must there be a Second Sex?
If Feminism's greatest goals
are liberated gender roles
then Gender we presume as given—
it is the base from which we're driven.
This Woman then would constitute
the prosecutor of our suit
and she's the one politically
whom we are serving fervently
and She's the one we'd represent
with Feminism's argument.
Yet "Politics" is no sure term
nor "Representing" very firm.

Well Representing helps, it's true
to win a Civil Right or two
but it oppresses us as well.
A man-made mold or iron shell
it must distort what it would show
(at least that's how I read Rousseau).
But we have tried to represent
this Woman to her betterment —
to find a language or discourse
that we could use as a resource
to make this Gender visible
and make our protest critical.
Indeed there's some necessity
in razing visibility
since Woman's life is not presented
in ways with which we're well contented.
And so it seems we need a Woman —
the a priori Subject given.
Yet Woman is no longer stable —
a term whose standing's now ill-able —
because there is of course debate
on what by "Woman" we'd relate
for surely there aren't Absolutes
nor Truth that "Woman" constitutes.

Now first of all there is some doubt
on what the Subject's all about.
I'm sure by now that you will know
the theories of Michel Foucault,
who claims that Power will create

the Subjects it would subjugate.
This Power works by prohibition,
by regulation, limitation
and discipline for our protection
(perhaps with choices and election)
and so its Subjects are controlled
as Power shapes them in its mold,
for it defines and then produces
these Subjects for its certain uses.
If this be true then we must ask
what is the "Subject" of our task?

If Feminism takes as given
that there are Subjects known as women,
how can we trust this formulation
that's simply Power's machination?
In fact the Subject whom we'd free
is Power's Subjectivity.
This system made those very Subjects
according to its rules, and its checks
dictate those terms, so we will find
that we are caught up in a bind.

The Subject is the question crucial.
It is to Feminism central
because the Subject is included
by what is otherwise excluded.
It is created by Repression
and so it makes up our Oppression.
The chains that bind it once it's rationed

hide beneath the form that's fashioned.
Repressive practices don't "show"
(at least that's how I read Foucault).
And so the Subject's a construction
that's made by Politics' production.
And when we think of Politics
in terms of States and their Subjects,
we would conceal the operations
of Power and its own relations.
The legal forces must invent
the Subjects whom they'd represent.
The Law produces and conceals
the Subject who to Law appeals.
This "Subject before Law" is prized
as premise that is naturalized —
this process magnificently
making Law's legitimacy.
And so it's not enough to try
correcting Patriarchy's lie
by finding ways to represent
this Woman with good faith intent
by showing literarily
this Subject more compellingly.
For we must also undertake
a study of the things that make
this Woman as a Category
and Subject whose goals liberatory
we would support, but who's produced
by structures we've not yet deduced.

So when we ask about this Subject
who stands before the Law's strict compact
now we must entertain the thought
that actually the Subject's not.
Perhaps it is just fictional,
a myth or construct cynical?

The Law makes fables that would trick us,
ascribing reality status
to Law and its dutiful subjects
who stand before the Law's strict precepts.

The Feminists who speak of women
would act as if one thing is given,
and yet the term is hardly stable —
to mean one thing it is ill-able —
nor can command the strong assent
of those whom it would represent.
For what we would a Woman call
is more than that, since it's not all —
not everything that she would be.
The term's not used exhaustively
and Gender is not constituted
coherently but convoluted
particular to Time and Place,
to Class or else to different Race.
For clearly Gender intersects
with Race and Class and Creed and Sex
and every which Identity
we formulate discursively!

And so it's not yet possible
to keep this Gender in control.
It's caught in many intersections
and mired in interconnections.
For Feminism then the case is
there's no one universal basis.
And there is no Identity
that can exist cross-culturally.

To say it somewhat with more candor:
there's not just one form of Oppressor.
A patriarchy universal
as concept isn't all that useful
because so many different contexts
there are in which Oppression exists.
Nor can we look at the specifics
to find examples of our concepts,
thus making them illustrations
of principles that beg our questions.

We're quick to label as one status
the Patriarchy's weight upon us
in order that we show the wisdom
of the claims of Feminism.
So as a shortcut we created
a Woman who is dominated
by a force that's universal —
a Subject who is shared by all.

A universal Patriarchy
appears now like so much malarkey.
And yet this other concept—Woman—
is waiting still to be disproven.
Can Woman ever preexist
Oppressor's grinding her to grist?
Or is it just in nation States
where Woman as a group relates?
Will Woman always be defined
against and within male Mankind?
And is there any Feminine
that every Woman has within?
Some Essence that's not Masculine—
a Universal Feminine?
Within the Gender Binary
sits Woman in her finery
and yet without that boundary
no females have camaraderie.
Whatever specificity
accrues to Femininity
is cut off analytically
and ghettoized politically
from every which Identity
like Class and Race/Ethnicity
and so the so-called Unity
of Woman's Subjectivity
is filled with ambiguity
and riddled with disunity.
Of course the source of all its force?
Representational discourse!

Now has this sketch exploratory
destabilized the category
of Woman seen as seamless set
a notion we must now reject.
And these domains exclusionary
reveal of course the regulatory
consequences of the construction
when put to our emancipation.
Indeed there is much fragmentation
in Feminism's coalition
and even there's some opposition
from women whose representation
would never fit so seamlessly
in Feminist femininity.
If Feminism's the suggestion
that there is a Representation
for all of those Feminist Subjects
whom Feminism itself thus constructs,
then this has had the consequence
of failing those constituents
whom Feminism represents
not giving an accounting for
Representation's power hoard.

We can't appeal to Strategy
to justify this Category
as though for purposes strategic
this Woman needs must be our Subject.
All strategies will mean much more
than what they are intended for

and in this case exclusion might be
an unintended Exigency:
by having fixed a stable Subject,
Representation's a false project.

Of course we cannot just refuse
Representation. We must use
the Language and the Norms today
which make the field on which we play.
There is no place outside this locus.
Therefore its practice is our focus.
We must address in any event
what Marx termed "historical present"
and so within the present frame
our task will be to give a name
to features of the Binary
which would construct the Category
in structures now contemporary
which certain Selves would naturalize
and others would immobilize.

So now within our Politics
which some would call "post-feminist"
we must interrogate this given —
the subjects who are known as "women."
We must critique this entity
which is human Identity
and track the Genealogy
of Gender as Ontology.
Then with smarter formulation

we can advance representation.
We necessarily critique
the theory feminist and seek
escape from the necessity
of holding an Identity.
To pose a rhetorical question:
Isn't it actually the notion
of the category of Woman
that thwarts goals of Representation?
Or perhaps it's that the Construction
of the category of Woman
is made partly through regulation
and serves as a reification
of what is a gendered relation?
Is Gender's categorization
heterosexualization?
Is Feminism not contrary
to reify the category?
If Gender as a stable notion
can be no longer our foundation
then we must probe the nitty-gritty
and question Gender Identity.
Now if we make Identity
a problematic entity
then we might trace politically
what forces work juridically
and seek a Genealogy
of the very Ontology
and set out in our inquiry
to deconstruct the Binary
that forms the Gender category.

2

The Compulsory Order of Sex/Gender/Desire

But as we now critically question
the age-old category Woman,
the category's invocation
precludes perhaps Representation.
Now does it really make much sense
that all the Subjects it presents
would be constructed by exclusion
of those not granted its inclusion?
And what would be the real relations
of forms of Power's dominations
and forms as well of its exclusion
sustained by that Representation?
We talk of Woman's Unity
constructing Solidarity
supposing shared Identity

and yet we always must remember
the split between what's Sex and Gender.
Created we that fine distinction
to torque the ancient formulation
which claimed that one's Biology
would make a person's Destiny.
By separating Sex and Gender
we must indeed now reconsider
how it's in fact that culturally
that we're constructed sexually.
And so we know that always Gender
does not result from Sex; and neither
is Gender nearly quite so fixed
as naturally as we are sexed.
Therefore the Subject's Unity
is not made with impunity
but as it were ALWAYS ALREADY
contested even by the Body
with Gender's multiplicity
eschewing fixed Identity.
Then Sex is by definition
agent of Gender's deconstruction!
If Gender is just cultural
while Sex purely is natural
it isn't necessarily
that Gender follows naturally
but actually there is distinction
built right into the assumption.
If even Sex is Binary
it's not therefore necessary

that Man's construction perfectly
informs male bodies totally.
Perhaps the sexes seem to be
an opposition Binary
but there's no reason it'd be true
that Gender's numbered just at two.
A binary gender system
relies on the common wisdom
that Sex is merely a mirror
reflecting a natural Gender.
A Subject's own Identity
should not assume priority
since perhaps the Subject's formation
is buried in the wrong foundation.
For Feminism there's no Woman
for our way of Representation.

3

Gender:
The Circular Ruins of
Contemporary Debate

Is Gender what you have or be?
Is Gender just made culturally?
Could we construct it differently?
Is there a possibility
of any gender agency?
Is Gender's universal axis
then always framed as different Sexes?
And is there ever any Gender
that's to the gendered Subject prior?
Now some would say this very notion
of Gender as man-made construction
functions deterministically
or even syllogistically
encoding Bodies culturally

in meanings anatomically
assigned and coded passively
as though it weren't Biology
but forces awfully culturally
that thereby frame our destiny.
And then in Simone de Beauvoir
(within her classic oeuvre) are
these thoughts you may have read before:
A woman's not as woman born
but she becomes as she would learn.
Preceding Gender? There's an ego,
an Agent (whom we call Cogito)
who at some point takes on a Gender
and therefore might have picked the other.
Construction then is not a choice?
Or does compulsion steal one's voice?
And does compulsion come from Sex?
Or made as Culture so expects?

In fact there isn't any Body
which would not ALWAYS ALREADY be
encoded by us culturally
so that it's just fallaciously
some preordained Biology
is basis for Ontology.
It looks like Sex by definition
is Gender, which is a construction.
And then this issue of construction
must founder on the rock, convention
debating if the Will has force

or if some Fate would Will coerce?
Given then such characteristics,
it all is traced back to Linguistics:
how our debate is so constrained
because (as I have just explained)
the Body's written in these terms
receiving as a set of Norms
a Will that is appropriative
or otherwise interpretative —
and so the Body's made to fit
the meanings inscribed onto it.
The Body too is a construction,
its meaning *post hoc* through deduction.
And neither does it exist ever
as prior to that marker Gender.
Therefore critiquing insistence
that the Body has existence
both in and through this mark of Gender
we simply cannot any longer
assume the Body's neatly filled
with Essence or that it's instilled
with whatsoever Self has willed.
So have not we discovered whether
it's either Sex or either Gender
that's firstly fixed, or is it free?
Or what if what it's seen to be
is actually a limitation
and just a pre-fab supposition
which is some claim of Humanism
wrecking all our radicalism?

Now this intractability
in the impossibility
of truly analyzing Gender —
because it's really made by Culture —
exposes there's a quandary
where Discourse builds a boundary
that's set within a Hegemonic
constructing system so Platonic
which degrades corporeality
and promotes rationality
since Language always will constrain
all Being to its own domain
(with Gender acting as its Name).
But whether Gender's cultural
or if it's biological
or if it is linguistical
ALWAYS ALREADY it's sexual —
an assumed Signification
that is put in a relation
of a kind of opposition
against some certain kind of Other
who would partake a different Gender.

Though Gender is relational
it's not ergo just personal;
because the Universal Person
is set against the other Woman
since Woman always is the Bearer
who carries with her marks of Gender

while Manliness and Personhood
are simply One — it's understood.

And yet to add a complication:
there is a deeper contradiction
which we might call a paradox;
though Sex is Woman, she's the Sex
who is not One (I do not lie:
I read it in Irigaray).
All Words are phallologocentric
and so the Masculine Linguistic
means Woman is not thinkable:
a Sex un-representable
who is a Multiplicity
illegible to Unity.

And then in Simone de Beauvoir
(within her classic oeuvre) are
these thoughts you may have read before:
the Woman always is the Other
who is the very mark of Gender.
According to Irigaray
(whom I cite true and do not lie)
the Woman cannot signify.

And so it's dialectically
that excluded entirely
is this Other's Identity
denied in Sign's economy
so that metaphysically

imposed is the Hegemony
that structures Subjectivity.

And yet what is the Metaphysics
presumed to be the Subject's substance?
And who is it shaping this complex
of the Sex and the Gender matrix?
Alas the humanistic concept
of the human as a so-called Subject
assumes that there's a Person
(or as it were a singular human)
who is an agent of an action
who's got a certain character
which forms within a basic core
upon which is a Gender, or
there's someone whom we'd call a Person
whom we deem capable of Reason
who simply has some attributes
now added onto Human roots.
This universalist conception
that views the Human as a Person
provides a point for our departure
in theorizing social Gender.
If Gender's really a position
constructed within a relation
among Subjects whose Construction
supplies their social constitution
and Gender follows that relation,
then Persons cannot simply "be"
except as they are socially.

And Essence must be relative
to that discourse relations give
and discourse more determinative
and Gender's then not substantive
but formed by discourse cultural
and, too, by terms historical.

And therefore the Feminine Sex
is only linguistic Absence—
the frank impossibility
of any such grammatically
named Noun which is substantively
not really a Reality.
According to Irigaray
whom I would cite without a lie,
it's actually her point of view
to show such Substance isn't true
but merely is a social force
produced my Masculine Discourse.
This Absence isn't marked as such—
an argument that very much
opposes what de Beauvoir's thought
(that Woman's marked and Man is not).
Irigaray's Sex is not Other—
the lack that defines the Male Gender.
The Feminine therefore can't be
defined thus theoretically
since Language would be phallocentric;
the Female Sex is not a Subject
and there is no representation

for any female/male relation
if linguistic economy
is made by Masculinity.

Between any social positions
we surely can make some distinctions
on what is perceived as the Subject
within the given social context.
The very circularity
of Feminism's inquiry
is underscored by the positions
which locate Gender inside Persons
and those who claim the very notion
which views the Human as a Person
who is positioned as a Subject
within the sexist pre-modern construct
without the possibility
both structurally, semantically,
of female positivity.

And then in Simone de Beauvoir
(within her classic oeuvre) are
these thoughts you may have read before:
the very notion of the Subject
within the existential project
which takes shape from Misogyny
is therefore ALWAYS ALREADY
a Masculine, a Universal
within the framework existential
defined precisely as it'd differ

from what it makes its female Other
outside its universal Norms
in singular, embodied forms.

Some say de Beauvoir wants to fight
for Woman, so she'll have the right
to be a Subject existential
in these same terms now universal.
But she rejects a cool Abstract
and disembodied, male Subject
as well as the disparagement
of disavowed embodiment
projected on the Feminine
as though the body's Female. Then
to link corporeality
somehow with Femininity
as a gesture just restricts
the Body and the Female Sex
as if it follows logically
however paradoxically:
Man is Incorporeality
and tool of Rationality
who only then is ever free.
And so de Beauvoir's proposition
would seem to start to beg the question:
Exactly what is this negation
by which male identification
is all Universality
and makes Corporeality
construed as Femininity?

The Master-Slave dialectic
provides some terms analogic
for this Gender asymmetry
prefiguring an Economy
that signs for Masculinity,
creating always its very Subject
in terms of course of this self-same lack.

And then in Simone de Beauvoir
(within her classic oeuvre) are
these thoughts you may have read before:
whether some Femininity
is an instrumentality
of Freedom and of Existence
or limiting as an Essence
which shows that the Embodiment
informing all her argument
is actually the reproduction
of old Descartes and his distinction
of Body as different from Freedom
yet I assert the contrary
against the ancient binary
which sets up that duality
of Mind and Body hierarchy—
where de Beauvoir sees as synthesis
in her compelling analysis
and claims this very dualism
would follow Phallocentrism.

Tradition philosophical
through Plato, Sartre, or Husserl
insists on the distinctiveness
of Body against Consciousness.
This slash between the body, soul
in Plato, Sartre, or Husserl
supports regimes political
as well as psychological
that thus are hierarchical:
For what by Dualism is meant
but fleeing from Embodiment?
And scholars now can document
the many texts that represent
the Mind as Masculinity,
the Body, Femininity.
So every single Reproduction
of Mind and Body in distinction
repeated thus conventionally
creates a Gender hierarchy.
But in de Beauvoir's formulation
there is always this separation
of Freedom and the human Body —
a Mark that's frankly shoddy
because it's not along the axis
of Gender and the Sexes —
but an old Cartesian distinction
in dire need (I think) of revision.
De Beauvoir's point officially
is that this Femininity
is marked on Body by Discourse

then leaves men's bodies (but of course)
unmarked as though universal;
but what is seemingly worse still:
according to Irigaray
(and yet again I do not lie),
the Marked is always like the Marker
so Self is always like the Other;
thereafter all Signification
is man-made and (as a construction)
puts Woman as an Otherness
and cannot grasp the differences
but gives a Label or a Name
and therefore marks it as the same.

4

Theorizing the Binary, the Unitary, and Beyond

De Beauvoir and Irigaray
don't either of them ever lie
but differ each in how they see
the patterns forming structurally
in Gender's own asymmetry.
For one, it's dialectically
in misfired reciprocity.
To the other, it's dialectic
hiding what's monologic.
The epistemological
as well as ontological
and even system logical
are by Irigaray exposed.
And yet whatever else she shows
is undercut: analysis

has failed in its ambitiousness.
For can we just identify
economies that signify
both always monolithically
as well as monologically,
transcending terms made culturally
as they are made historically
in many different far-flung contexts
which each have differences of Sex?
For is it not Imperialism
or even like Phallocentrism
to ignore all the operations
of different ways there are Oppressions?
To simply note the many cultures
as other kinds of othered Others
is another amplification
of the very same, tired construction
and again an appropriation
(maybe an unthought repetition)
and gesture of colonization
by which the Phallus, too, would function.

Of course as Feminists we seek
to explicate and to critique
manly claims so totalizing
even in our own theorizing.

To name just one Identity
of a singular enemy
also mimics the strategy

of Masculine Patriarchy
and doesn't offer any more
than terms of the Oppressor, or
if such totalizing tactics
would work well in both these contexts
then such gestures colonialist
are not then purely masculinist
but can texture any relation
with a hint of subordination.

Nor yet can we make the assumption
that there is one discrete Oppression
that has a sequential existence
along a certain model axis
that has a structure horizontal
and thus ignores all factors social.
Nor may we use another model
that takes a shape that's vertical
that would rank different Oppressions
in groups of causal-linked relations
presuming some originations,
preserving thereby derivations.
The field of Power whose structure
is the colonial gesture
encompasses also the axis
of differences of the Sexes
so that its very differential
is not at all hierarchical
in terms of Phallocentrism
or Racism or Classism,

each stemming from some first position
as though the primary condition
of originary oppression.
And so the false appropriation
of an Other's own suppression
is never just exclusively
enjoined by Masculinity.

Now these debates in Feminism
that dwell on an Essentialism
raise many a pertinent question
about a Masculine Oppression
and universal claims to free
a Feminist Identity.
Well any universal claim
takes as its standpoint that old same
and shared Epistemology
which simply makes apology
for some outdated Unity
ascribed to Femininity
as being Sexuality
and linked up with Maternity.
To me the globalizing gesture
(already I've said in this chapter)
has generated quite a number
of critiques quite admonitory
of Gender as a category
and Woman as exclusionary
when she is seen as unitary
and this negates entirely

the full, rich multiplicity
— intersections politically
and socially and culturally —
and fits them all in one construction
and patly labels it a "woman."

Some thinkers seek a formulation
of Feminism's coalition
which won't assume essentially
what always Woman needs must be.
And so the identification
of those who are in that position
sometimes articulated as Woman
might join to foster coalition.
Now clearly this coalitional
transformation is political
and yet the form of coalitions
(assemblages of new positions)
cannot be set, not pre-determined
without inviting inadvertent
problems caused by limitation
on shaping a new coalition.
Insisting on a Unity
assumes that Solidarity
is somehow purely fundamental
to any action instrumental.
And yet perhaps the coalition
could well accept a contradiction
and see inherent fragmentation
furthering democratization.

Might not it be that Dialog
is really just a Monolog
that is specific culturally
and bound to historicity?
And therefore the Power relations
which fuel such basic limitations
on working dialogically
require, too, our scrutiny
(or else the dialogic model
would recapitulate the liberal
assumption always of some equal
who as a Subject must agree
on what would count as Unity).
But it is just a fallacy
to invoke Woman, as though she
is solely one Identity
or Class, Age, Race/Ethnicity
and of one Sexuality.

And so by making the assumption
about the baked-in incompletion
that allows that category
to be open permanently—
as an ideal that is normative
without its being demonstrative—
we ask if it is necessary
to attain any unitary
solidarity as a goal
for each action political?
Is not all such regimentation

the cause or root of fragmentation?
Might not it be that coalition
might better pursue desired action
embracing at once fragmentation
against that very Unity
of Woman as Identity?

The Norm of Solidarity
promotes an exclusivity
at level of Identity
excluding possibility
of every set of proposed actions
which might well cause disliked disruptions
to break out at the very border
that's between the Self and its Other.

This Unity indeed as goal
is always just conceptual
and Unity's provisional—
in every form contextual
not bearing any expectation
that every Feministic action
must now arise in Unity
of one same fixed Identity.
And action then could now begin
as every which and way, "women"
excluded once, can now join in.
And this anti-foundational
approach that's coalitional
as a new form political

assumes neither Identity
nor any so-called Unity.

Advancing thus Identity
in Culture's terms of Unity
instates always a definition
preventing thereby the creation
of any identity concepts
new-made in political actions.
So any call to Unity
cannot expand Identity.

But when the old Identities
and representing entities
no longer are only the Subject
which fuels our political project,
well then can new Identities
arise in new exigencies.
Certain political practices
now arranged on new-found axises
devised on a contingent basis
can come about then as the case is.
So a structural political
that now is coalitional
need not expand the category
to make it somewhat unitary
but offers more complexity
to Self as multiplicity.

If Gender's a complexity
whose claim to a totality
is ALWAYS ALREADY deferred
(its self-same essence not affirmed)
then to affirm Identity
conflicting in disunity
allows structure that is hodge-podge
of sundry, open assemblage
permitting both convergences
as well as those divergences
that without Telos normative
denies closure definitive.

5

Identity, Sex,
and the Metaphysics of Substance

Oh! what is an Identity?
And what can ground the certainty
Identities are actual
and all are self-identical
persisting, as though they're the same—
coherent, single, with one name?
And even more importantly
does Gender have Identity?
We can't discuss Identity
unless we make an inquiry
into something that comes prior
which of course is human Gender
since never are there human Persons
except as we are gendered constructs.

It seems to me now that the notion
of Human Being as a Person
(as one who has some agency)
makes claims to an Ontology—
an argument about the Being
implicit in one's social Meaning.
And yet this takes elaboration
and questioning of the assumption
that actually the context social
exists outside (as an external)
with somehow a true Personhood
either already understood
as Consciousness or else as Reason
or as moral deliberation.
The question of Identity
is (within most Philosophy)
almost always one centered on
some internal criterion
presuming continuity
to Self as one Identity
(of just one Person throughout Time).
But such conjectures are not mine.

Instead I ask to what degree
do regulations that we see
as Gender's social formulation—
constructing its dualist division—
not constitute Identity
creating in reality
the mere coherence of Subjects

with their self-identical status?
Is it not that Identity
derives from Normativity
assigned as if it comes from Nature
when it's a descriptive feature?
In other words Identity
when seen as Continuity
is not a tick of Personhood
(as is thus often understood)
but it's a trick made socially
by norms constructed culturally
of intelligibility
dictating legibility.

In as much as Identity
is linked to Sexuality
as well as Sex and Gender norms
then in the way the Person forms
there is a problematic question
which is open to a decontsruction.
And now we track the emergence
of beings whose supposed coherence
appears to make them Persons, but
their Gender makes us wonder what
their essence is, which won't conform
to any culture's Gender norm
by which the Person is defined —
so we are caught up in a bind.

Genders are intelligible
and somehow they are integral
to structures institutional—
coherences relational—
maintaining their continual
Identities as Sexual
as Gendered and Desirable.
In other words there are Specters
of discontinuous vectors
produced and then prohibited
by Laws which all have limited
a Gender to perceived connection
of linking Sex with its Expression.

And yet by now I'm sure you know
that that's the point made by Foucault.
For as he ironically terms it
Sex's truth is made by the norms it
itself makes as Identity
in forming Sexuality.
Well Heterosexualization
always makes the instantiation
of a discursive opposition
between what's seen as Feminine
and what's construed as Masculine
(where these two terms are understood
as attributes of Personhood).
And yet the culture gives the Norms
by which all gendered selves have forms
and Norms require and insist

that selves can only then exist
when Gender follows from its Sex
as well when gender practices
should follow normatively either
the custom of their Sex or Gender:
Identity's relational
to structures, which (political
and made by the customs cultural)
would shape our sexualities.

Since some Gender Identities
must fail already to conform
to suit the letter of the norm
they seem impossibilities
or as it were monstrosities.
And yet these rare Identities
provide us opportunities
to open up the very terms
of identitarian norms.

When Identity is legible
and therefore it's intelligible,
that's when the matrix singular
creates it own peculiar
deep link within compulsory
Heterosexuality's
discursive regularities
that make up Sex Identities.
Identity's made by the force
of Power ruled through its Discourse.

Then is Gender Identity
not made by regulatory
and erstwhile a compulsory
Heterosexuality?

Or would maybe that explanation
actually be totalization
where Heterosexuality
just takes the place that logically
was held by Phallocentrism
as sole cause of all Sexism?

We learn from France whose Feminists
as well as her Post-Structuralists
make no agreement uniform
that would define that "Power" term.
Consider all the oppositions
among the various positions.
We have at first—I would not lie—
the views of Luce Irigaray
who says there is no Sex but One
(the Masculine whose production
opposes any other Gender
which simply is the male one's Other.
And then as you are sure to know
there is the point made by Foucault
who sees both Masculinity
as well as Femininity
and even Sexuality
as all one single entity

built up by discursivity
of science and modernity.
And then of course I'd not renege
the work of one Monique Wittig
who keys Sex as a category
to the regime regulatory
of the condition compulsory
of Heterosexuality
constructed as the Feminine
by universal Masculine.
But Wittig as you surely know
agrees in essence with Foucault
that Sex will end when finally we
o'erthrow what's the Hegemony
of Heterosexuality.

These models each explanatory
show Sex as a category
but understood in different terms
of Power in its many forms.
So what's the possibility
that we can think complexity
of all these fields of power, or
how all them mash together; for
the theory of sexual difference
suggests that there's no real existence
granted the Female as a Subject
because she's totally the Object
within a representational
program or system conventional.

She's always the Representation
and hence without representation.
Irigary's Ontology
then argues somewhat subtly
a Woman's what can't simply be
because she is the very Difference
who's baked already into Essence —
she's not just the Opposite Sex
in contrast to manly Subjects
nor's she just the Opposite Gender
opposed to the Masculine Other —
she's really the economy
of Opposition's binary
(the secret, monologic plan
who's used constructing human Man).

Yet all agree despite difference
that Language makes from Sex Substance
or a self-identical Being
as though not a way of seeing.
Discourse conceals! We cannot be
a Sex or Gender essentially.
So now again I do not lie
when I say that Irigaray
would claim that Grammar's no index
of what is Gender or is Sex
for Grammar privileges the model
of Gender as the foundational
and Binary in opposition
between — within — representation.

Irigaray says that this Grammar
(subtending to its take on Gender)
assumes that Man and Masculine
and Woman and the Feminine
create a kind of Binary
which masks a higher harmony—
the singular Hegemony
of one sole Masculinity
that shuts up Femininity
as site of Multiplicity
against the Phallic Unity.

Also by now I'm sure you know
that Sex's Grammar for Foucault
imposes the Gender Binary
through a system regulatory
shrinking the Multiplicity
of any Sexuality
that might disrupt Hegemony.

Yet nor would I ever renege
on noting how Monique Wittig
examines Sex's Binary
in terms of a compulsory
Heterosexuality
and aims to squash that tyranny—
advancing a true Humanism
that's free from any rank sexism.
And elsewhere she views the promotion,
the profusion, indeed diffusion,

of all economies erotic
that are not strictly phallocentric
as ways that we might flatly free
Sex, Gender, and Identity.
And Wittig sees the Lesbian
as pushing back from restriction
of any Gender Binary
imposed by Sexuality.

But in her humanist assumption
the modes of all signification
as well as all representation
are not under interrogation.
But rather self-determination
affects the rehabilitation
of existential agency
granted to Lesbianity.
Therefore she won't critique the Subject
who is Patriarchy's Symbolic.
Effectively her argument
negotiates some replacement
of the universal Subject, Man
with a new one, the Lesbian.
So the Woman-Is-Sex equation
is just a Masculine conflation
encoding Femininity
as sexed Corporeality—
hence, a refusal to grant women
the freedom that's granted men.

To break Sex as this property
might phase out the misogyny
which makes Sex a synecdoche
for all of Femininity.

Gender Wittig sees as index
for the old opposition, Sex,
and claims there only is one Gender
which is used always in singular
where the Masculine is general
as a non-gendered Universal.
And Wittig calls for the destruction
of Sex as made by this construction
where Woman must assume the status
of Subjecthood that is denied us.
As we move toward that destruction
the Woman still must somehow function
as universal point of view
and as particular one, too.
So Wittig's view of the Lesbian
(replacing her in the Subject, Man)
confirms the normative promise
of Metaphysics of Substance
(the ideals of Humanist ethics).

So Wittig does not quite comply
with insights from Irigaray
but she defends that the presumed Person
who's equated perhaps with Freedom
assuming a status pre-social

for a freedom that's universal,
subscribing as well in essence
to a Metaphysics of Substance
responsible for the production
of Sex as a hidden construction.

Well the Metaphysics of Substance
is something that scholars would nuance
in discussions contemporary
of Nietzschean philosophy.
And in setting out to teach me
about works by Friedrich Nietzsche,
says Harr: the methodology
for building up Ontology
is trapped in Illusions of Being—
in fallacious, dumb ways of seeing—
mistaking Grammar's prerequisite
of the Subject and the Predicate
as though they were Reality
of some one true Identity
at levels of Ontology
(of Substance and of Attribute)—
Constructions Wittig would dispute
because they serve to institute
an Order and Simplicity
in some one true Identity.
They don't present and can't reveal
an Order that is really Real.

This criticism Nietzschean
explains the pickle we are in:
psychological categories
govern at last the theories
of Gender and Identity
and give to them Reality.
For Haar and for other such critics
this is a false Metaphysics
and offers critique of the notion
of Psychological Person
who's viewed as a substantive thing
(or—if you prefer—like *das Ding*).
Psychological categories
derive from false preliminaries
(assumptions of Identities)
which is the belief in Language
with all of its messy baggage.

Now Grammar made Descartes presume
ego cogito ergo sum.
But does "I" think? No! Certainly!
The truth is that thoughts come to me.
Really the Subject's false conception
merely arises from the fiction
that any kind of Unity
begins in words' Reality.

And as Wittig has shown moreover
there isn't a Language sans Gender.
Wittig analyzes the Grammar

of French as it pertains to Gender
and through this work in Wittig's eyes
this Gender not only qualifies
but constitutes the Episteme
by which this Gender we would deem
as somehow universalized.
(Although of course Wittig realized
it's not the same in French and English
this gendering grammatical-ish.)
Nevertheless the mark of Gender
is always just as Grammar's rendered
with Person always as a bearer
linguistically as some one Gender—
a primitive Ontology
that is a built-in Binary.
Arising from Ontology
this Gender is Philosophy.
And Wittig's views corroborated
by discourses so saturated
with implicit Ontology
in Sex and Sexuality.

The claim that one may simply be
a Sex or Sexuality
is clearly symptomatical
of Western metaphysical
assumptions about Substances
where Genders seem as Essences.
And in the case of men and women
this would subordinate the notion

of Gender to Identity
and furthermore the fallacy
that Person can a Gender be
presumes some state of prior Essence
that's coupled with presumed existence
or sense of self-identity
that's linked to Sexuality.

In a pre-feminist context
which would confuse Gender with Sex
Gender's a mode of Unity
for embodied Identity
opposed to some Sex Opposite
whose structure's a prerequisite
to build an oppositional
coherence individual
among Desire, Sex, and Gender,
inside a Self that they each render.

Assumption that one just can be
a given, sexed Anatomy
is undermined by observation
of gendered psychic disposition.
"I feel like a Woman" is true
because Aretha has sung "You
make me feel." So always the Other
invoked is an opposite Gender —
a formulation that coerces
the Binary it thus imposes.

Gender can be a Unity
of Sex and Sexuality
only when Sex is understood
as equal to what Gender would
and only when Desires be
Heteronormativity—
performed in terms of a relation
where Sex is made in opposition.
Indeed for Gender's Unity
there ALWAYS ALREADY needs must be
Heterosexuality.

Heterosexuality
produces uniformity
of gendered terms that constitute
a Binary we must refute.

Well there is a presupposition
within this very Gender relation
of a casual reproduction
of Sex and Sexuality
for Gender is Desire, or
Desire's Gender. Furthermore
within this certain Unity
constructed metaphysically
Sex, Gender, Sexuality—
with each one in this Trinity
now all unlocked by just one key:
Heterosexuality.

A naturalistic paradigm
where Sex and Gender intertwine
with these in continuity
to lusting Sexuality
as basis of Identity
and for a paradigm expressive
which sees the Self as successive
to Sex and Gender and Desire
and not to such expression prior —
are both what Luce Irigary
(I paraphrase but do not lie)
sees as a wish to reify.

This sketch of Gender gives a clue
for the substantializing view
and its deeper Metaphysics
as linked to Power Politics.
The instutionality
of the rank compulsory
Heterosexuality
requires Gender's Binary
with one term, Masculinity
demarked from Femininity —
a demarcation overall
clearly Heterosexual.

And then this differentiation
of two intertwined oppositions
creates a strong consolidation
or a presumptive Unity

both within Masculinity
and in Femininity
through terms of Sexuality.

Now the displacement strategy
of relational Binary
form of its ontological stance
(the Metaphysics of Substance)
claims Gender's dueling categories
are made within its binaries.
And then I'm sure that you will know
that that's implicit in Foucault:
Sex, he says, as category
is product of an inventory
produced within Modernity
by modes of Sexuality.
And the strange, tactical production
of that old, discursive construction
of our Sex within a Binary
conceals of course the primary
aims of the secret apparatus
which postulates that both the Sexes
are cause of Sexuality.
Here's a conclusion that he draws:
"It is an effect that seems the cause."
Regimes of Sexuality
by functioning discursively
instate the Gender Binary
and thus make Sex a category.

In an intro Foucault would write
to notes by a hermaphrodite
(a certain Herculine Barbin
whose journals — in Foucault's jargon —
show "practices" that would critique
Modernity and its technique).
Heterosexuality —
which cannot grasp an Identity
that thwarts its Sexuality.

From norms this Herculine departs
having both male and female parts.
Moreso the system just has shelves
for filing certain gendered Selves.
And those conventions that produce
a Self in terms of Sex, reduce
the Self to either He or She —
a frame that Herculine'd exceed
since Herculine deploys the terms
of Gender using "both" its forms
and thus exceeds the finery
set up by Gender's Binary.
Conversing disconcertingly,
Heterosexuality
and Homosexuality
are advanced anatomically
in a discontinuity
of Heterogeneity
that's cut off paradoxically.
by "Hetero"-sexuality

(undermining subversively
that Metaphysics of Substance
once seen as the very Essence
of identitarian Sex).

Foucault sees Herculine's experience as some Pleasures that
are like the "grin" without the "cat!"
And Pleasures thus are figured here
as qualities that don't adhere
to any abiding Substance
which thus suggests the happenstance
of all gendered experience
not apprehended as Substance
or the hierarchical Grammar
of a Noun and Modifier.

Through this reading of Herculine
our Foucault claims that he has seen
exposure ontological
of attributes accidental
and postulates Identity
as restricted culturally
in principles of hierarchy.
And this insight wholly dispenses
with Genders any Substances
so it's no longer possible
to hold the gendered Subject whole
subsuming Gender dissonance
into a prior essence, as

if men might act quite Feminine
yet with some manly underpin
(a "man" who is Ontology
or figure of Biology).
But the notion of this Substance
is just a fictitious essence
produced through the compulsory
construction of coherency
which orders neatly Attributes
into the Gender Absolutes.

And so it seems this dissonance
must undermine the Substance stance.
Appearance of a Self that's gendered
is by a Regulation rendered
which marshals forced coherences
into some fictive Substances.
The exposure of this production
as made by Regulation
by resisting assimilation
with attributes, or any quirk
transgressing the same old framework
as certain dissonant Adjectives
would redefine the Substances
(the Nouns that they would modify).
And so we may hypothesi
that this explodes as forgeries
all of Gender's categories
since they include what they exclude
(as we quite rightly must conclude).

But if supposed Substances
are nothing but coherences
of contingently made construction,
of attribute in regulation,
then the very Ontology
is formed quite artificially
and so a superfluity.

So as this now is broken down
we see that Gender's not a Noun.
But neither is it made from sets
of some free-floating sobriquets.
We can't deny that its effect
is made within the old Subject
(mainly when performatively
it is imposed coercively
when Power wants coherency).

In Metaphysics of Substance
a Gender's merely Performance
which makes up that Identity
that Gender would presume to be.

In the terms that I'm construing
Gender simply is a Doing
and not the doing of a Subject
who before the Deed could exist.
In the project liberatory
of thinking the category —
outside Metaphyiscs of Subtance —

there is certainly relevance
for what some critics would teach me
about words by Friedrich Nietzsche.
"There is no Being just the Deed."

Now Nietzsche might not have agreed
but let me state a corollary:
There is no Gender category
and no Gender Identity
behind Performativity
and this makes the very expression
that's presumed to have been their Essence.

6

Language, Power,
and the Strategies of Displacement

But so many Feminist screeds
presume a Doer does the Deeds.
Unless at first an Agent be
it seems there'd be no Agency
and hence no mode of transformation
for protesting our domination.
But Wittig is ambiguous
when it comes down to these Subjects.
On one hand, Wittig would dispute
the metaphysic Absolute.
But on the other, she explains
the human Subject she retains
(the Agent individual
as locus metaphysical).
The Construction she diagnoses

but meanwhile she still presupposes
a Doer who's behind the Deed
and yet acknowledges the need
to know Gender's performative.

So the dispute that she would give
regards the temporality
of conflating fallaciously
the cause of Gender with results
so it's the Sequence that she faults.

And yes! by now I'm sure you know
that Wittig's sharing with Foucault
the trace of the old Marxist notion
of what's known as Reification:
she tells us that the major gist
of material-feminist
approaches to this problem show
(you know she echoes with Foucault)
that what appears as Origin
for the Oppressions we are in
is in fact like a mark imposed
within the Discourse of our foes.

The "Myth of Woman" manifests
only through a False Consciousness.
And thus this mark can't pre-exist:
Oppression marks out what Sex is
and tells that our Sex be taken
as *a priori* Subject given.

So Sex, which looks like true perception
is really just a myth's construction;
and meanwhile, yet the Oppressor
proclaims that Sex is like Nature
(according to Compulsory
Heterosexuality).

For Wittig, the Homosexual
is a proposition radical —
a desire liberatory
who would transcend the category.
So Sex can't simply be erased
or obfuscated or effaced
by contesting effectively
Heterosexuality.

But when I cite Irigaray?
Believe you me! I do not lie.
She argues flatly: Gender's mark
must be seen the crucial part
that operates foundationally
in the field of Ontology.
For Wittig, Language is a tool
whose structures metaphysical
are in no way misogynist —
only the application is.

Irigaray would like to see
somehow the possibility
of a new sign Economy

that might escape the Mark of Gender
which in fact is the erasure
by the Phallologocentric
of the Female from its rubric.

Irigaray says: Binary
excludes all Femininity.
And Wittig claims that this position
is the re-consolidation
of the old, sexist mythic fiction.

Drawing on Simone de Beauvoir
(within whose classic oeuvre are
some thoughts you may have read before),
Wittig says that there's no such thing
as writing that is Feminine.
For Wittig, there is no debate
that Language serves to subjugate
but in her methodology
she views all words materially
with words even an institution
that might portend a Revolution.
Language is a concrete practice
maintaining the very actions
of Individuals, and hence
weakening by the consequence
of concerted collective action
from within the linguistic Fiction.

If the category of Sex
(as Wittig astutely suggests)
is produced as a category
by the framework of mandatory
Heterosexuality—
to always restrict Identity
along a normative axis
of the two opposing Sexes,
Homosexuality
may overthrow Hegemony
of Sex as a category.

But Wittig also takes an issue
with using Genital Tissue
organizationally
to construct us sexually—
as an Economy
that counters Subjectivity
marked by Woman's supposedly
distinct, natural Gender function
in Sexual Reproduction.

Now all this great proliferation
of pleasure through Imagination
suggests a Feminine formation
of Eros's certain diffusion
as though opposed to the construction
of supposed Genitality.

In a sense the Lesbian Body
is an inverted kind of theory
of Freud's old Sexuality
which claimed superiority
of Phallic Sexuality
(over former Anality
and polymorph Perversity).
Only an Invert (in Freud's terms)
fails to reach the Genital norms.
Critiquing Genitality
Inversion is used critically
and praised by Wittig (precisely
as that one Sexuality
operating politically
as a post-genitality).

In Heterosexism's Matrix
the development of the Sexes
is always their Normalization.
And so Wittig's mobilization
as well as radical subversion
of this old, Freudian Inversion
may just however reinscribe
the structure she would undermine.

If every anti-genital
is seen as oppositional
into the structure sexual
then would not then the Binary
just reproduce quite endlessly?

Well the psychoanalysis
of which Wittig's opponent is
produced as a consequence
a double bind, since in a sense
she assumes in her argument
Freud's theory of development
which although it's now "inverted"
isn't therefore just subverted.

So Polymorph Perversity
assumed as being primary
before the added Mark of Sex
is then in Wittig's work expressed
as being highest in degree
of human Sexuality.
(Perhaps she underestimates
how Language always propagates
the Mark of Gender, which she'd label
disposable and variable.)

In the Lacanian theory
a prohibition primary
would operate more forcefully
and really less contingently
than practice regulatory
like the kind of category
which by now I am sure you know
is theorized by Michel Foucault.

In Lacan (I do not lie)
it's just as in Irigaray:
Sex is not a category
that is formed in a Binary
which would retain as its basis
a Substantive Metaphysics
but it is a fictive construction —
i.e., the Masculine Subject —
produced when Father's Law prohibits
every desire of Incest,
forcing the Heterosexual
into timeless deferral.

The Female's never just a mark
or attitude or added part.
The Feminine is like a lack
on which the Law will then unpack
a set of different rules linguistic
that's signified by the Symbolic
creating the Sexual Difference
giving Lacanian inference:
that by the Founding Prohibition
does the masculinist position
have individualization —
a heterosexualization
of and through the Law of the Father
which would bar the Son from Mother
so ever even their relation
is also an Instantiation
of that same old Law of the Father

(whereas always a girl's desire
for both her Father and her Mother
requires that she be the bearer
of the mark of Maternity).
So both male Masculinity
as well as Femininity
are instituted from within
the prohibitions that produce
such Subjects for their certain use
so Genders made unconsciously
emerge in an Imaginary
of Gendered Sexuality.

The appropriation Feminist
of the Sexual Difference
attempts to see the Feminine
but not as it's been grounded in
a Metaphysics of Substance
but just as a wordless Absence
affected by the male rejection
which grounds all Signification
(indeed through this very exclusion).

The Feminine as Excluded
within that frame (it is concluded)
betrays the possibility
of shaking the Hegemony.

The works of Gallop and of Rose
in different ways would both propose

the same very constructed status
of all the Sexual Difference —
its basic instability
and consequent duality
of the same Law whose point would be
the Sexual Identity.

Now Wittig in the French context
would argue that the Difference
is actually a replication
of an old abstraction.

This neglects unconscious realms
in which Repression overwhelms:
emerging in the Essences
it undercuts coherences.
As Rose points out (and I agree)
a construction of Identity
along the disjunctive axis
of the Male and the Female sexes
is bound to fail. Yes! the Repressed
emerges. And when it's expressed
reveals the Self's constructedness:
Prohibition's Identity
must fail at self-same Unity.
Paternal Law's a bumbling whim
who aids us in o'erthrowing him!

The differences that now emerge
within these Schools — as they diverge —

regard a quarrel over whether
one now can ever just recover
some Sexuality before
the Law, or in Self's true core
or after Law, post-genital.
(But then it's paradoxical
that Polymorph Perversity
in both views theoretically
trumps any Sexuality.)

Yet no agreement here at all
about the nature of the Law:
the psychoanalytic Subject
would be produced within the Matrix
conjoining with elusive Substance.

Wittig's existentialism
assumes an essentialism:
there's a Subject who's pre-social
yet it seems the Law paternal
is really quite less unitary
than Structuralist Imaginary.

But the quarrel seems to turn on
the ancient articulation —
subversive Sexuality
of unknown temporality.
It grows before the Law's imposed?
Or after Law has been opposed?
Or during Law in constant fight?

Now it seems here we should invite
an insight, which I'm sure you know
derives from old Michel Foucault
who claims that Sexuality
is Power's own Ancillary
(against a naïve postulation
of any great Emancipation
of some new Sexuality
which from the Law somehow is Free).

But we must argue after all
that both "before" and "after" Law
are modes of temporality
and each is made discursively
and each involved within the terms
of Hegemony's wicked norms.
So there's no radicality
in any Sexuality
that could escape the reigning Lex
of prohibitions around Sex.

And, too, by now I'm sure you'll know
such prohibitions (says Foucault)
would make the Subject — whose production
is of and in this prohibition —
could have no Sexuality
but Power's Subjectivity.
For Power rather than the Law
would saturate quite nearly all
though its differences relational

both productive and juridical.
And hence the Sexuality
as Power's Subjectivity
is not a simple replication
and not the Law's mere repetition
repeating Law's economy
of Masculine Identity.
To mute the possibility
of any Subjectivity
which thwarts intelligibility
expands then quite effectively
what's created culturally.

A Sex that is post-genital
has undergone some critical
and Feminist interpretation
and Lesbian appropriation
of post-sex Sexuality
that's purported to be free.

Through a process exclusionary
Power's pattern regulatory
restricts the meaning seen to be
Heterosexuality
and Homosexuality
and any sites of a Transgression
as well as resignification.

That both Heterosexism
and Phallologocentrism

augment themselves through repetition
of ontological position
and even of their inner logic
and thereby their own metaphysic —
this does not always just imply
that Repetition ought to die.
If Repetition must persist
within the way that we exist
as Culture's own Identities
then we must pose some inquiries
about what kind of repetition
might further as a new subversion
and call the System into question.
If there is Sex and Personhood
but only as they're understood
by Power as it dictates terms
for working only in its norms,
then what's the possibility
of holding the Identity
but playing with those terms' inversion
and acting out their own subversion?

Whereas Foucault's ambiguous
about how Power's practices
would play out so discursively
to produce a category
and Wittig says that the Construction
is joined to Human Reproduction
yet other forces help produce
the Subjects for their certain use

for reasons we can scarce deduce.
The Sciences are so infused
with Power and are so reduced.
And Medicine's conjoined with Law
in ways that aren't yet clear at all.

It seems to me discursively
there is so much complexity
to Gender's form as a construction —
a promise or an invitation?
How the regulatory fiction
facilitates its deconstruction!

Nor is it just a failed project
of critiquing the Law's compact
as if critique political
undoes the forces cultural.

If someone's Sexuality
is constructed culturally
within all Power's own relations
well then our very postulations
of any Sexuality
outside Power's Hegemony
are an impossibility
not practical politically
postponing the possibility
of thinking Sexuality
subverting its Identity

within the given set of terms
determined first by Power's norms.

Within such norms to operate
then would not simply replicate
uncritically the same relation
of Power with its domination.
Instead the Law in replication
might refuse all consolidation
and offer up a new subversion.
Rather than Sexuality
equal to Masculinity
and Phallus's proclivity
we can somewhat more playfully—
through subversive operation—
re-perform identification.

So if in Rose's explanation
any such identification
is truly (Rose says) phantasmatic
then really it's axiomatic
that one can perform Identity
in ways that show its fantasy.

If there's no exit radical
from its constructions cultural
it's still for us to ask the question
how one might act one's construction.
Are not there forms of repetition
that aren't just idle imitation

not merely social Reproduction
building up Law's consolidation?
But what are new configurations
and what convergent matrices
would undo these interstices?
The truth of Power's hierarchy
in modern Sexuality
is not the simple augmentation
of crystal-clear consolidation.
Since they're contested sites of meaning
Sex and Gender invite re-reading
as each is Multiplicity
holding the possibility
of working to subversively
perform their lack of Unity.

Proposing no Ontology
and no Phenomenology
I don't endeavor to lay out
what Gender's being's all about.
Yet I presume that to "be" Gendered
is just a construct that is rendered —
an object of investigation
that maps out Self as a construction
within the bounds political
in the mode ontological.

So to call Gender a "construction"
is not making any assertion
that it's ergo artificial

where this is oppositional
contending with Reality.
But as a Genealogy
I seek within this inquiry
to know that discursivity
within the plausibility
of the relational Binary.
And now I am eager to wager
that configurations of Gender
assert their own Reality
to augment their Hegemony.

And then in Simone de Beauvoir
(within her classic oeuvre) are
these thoughts you may have read before:
A woman's not as woman born
but she becomes as she would learn.
"Woman" simply marks the processes
of acting liminal statuses
without an end or origin
and therefore it always is open
to a radical intervention
as well as resignification.
Even when Gender would conceal
in forms that often may feel real,
well this congealing's simply social
not guided by some Telos final.

So Gender's just a repetition
or really a stylization—

a set of acts that over time
congeal along an ordered line
producing somehow appearance
of a Being with a Substance.

To do the genealogy
of Gender as Ontology
would deconstruct thus the Appearance
into such acts sans a Substance
and locate these acts within frames
built by Power for its own aims
conforming to the names it names.

To show as mere contingency
what seemed like a necessity
has been one of the major parts
of Criticism after Marx.

But now this task must intersect
with the Gender of all Subjects
admitting possibility
foreclosed by Power's policy
which structures its Ontology.

So later my analysis
investigates the Structuralist
account of Difference Sexual
as this may still prove possible
contesting modes of Power, for
the presumed coherence of Gender

and sex's univocity
(within the system binary)
are now revealed as idle fictions
which just allow consolidations
of Power's Masculinity
and Heterosexuality.

Also we must view the Body
not as such a surface ready
to receive Signification
but a scene of a contestation —
a blurry set of boundaries
controlled by Power's functionaries.

No! Sex is not Identity
but a performativity
which is in fact not a "to be."

And when Gender has been denaturalized
and its social construction realized
and the terms of Gender re-mobilized
so that the terms that once had crystallized
even in the Feminist enterprise
can now all be somehow re-stylized
then can Gender Trouble be strategized,
reconfigured, performed, and satirized.

❧

A.W. Strouse teaches medieval literature at The New School. Strouse is the author of *My Gay Middle Ages* (punctum books, 2015) and *Transfer Queen* (punctum books, 2018).

Made in the USA
Middletown, DE
17 August 2020